EVERYBODY ALWAYS

BOB GOFF

EVERYBODY ALWAYS

BECOMING LOVE *in a*
WORLD FULL *of* SETBACKS
and DIFFICULT PEOPLE

· · · · · · · · · · · · · ·

S T U D Y   G U I D E

NELSON
BOOKS

An Imprint of Thomas Nelson

Published in Nashville, Tennessee, by Thomas Nelson. Thomas Nelson is a registered trademark of HarperCollins Christian Publishing, Inc.

Published in association with the literary agency of Alive Communications, Inc. www.alivecommunications.com.

All Scripture quotations, unless otherwise indicated, are taken from *The Holy Bible, New International Version®, NIV®*. Copyright © 1973, 1978, 1984, 2011 by Biblica, Inc.™ Used by permission. All rights reserved worldwide.

Thomas Nelson titles may be purchased in bulk for educational, business, fundraising, or sales promotional use. For information, please e-mail SpecialMarkets@ThomasNelson.com.

ISBN 978-0-310-09533-0

First Printing March 2018 / Printed in the United States of America

CONTENTS

INTRODUCTION

"Love the Lord your God with all your heart and with all your soul and with all your strength and with all your mind"; and, "Love your neighbor as yourself."

LUKE 10:27

Welcome to *Everybody, Always*!

It's good that you're here. Like, really good. Because the world we're living in right now is really good at something else: division. It is great at teaching us to only trust people who talk like us, think like us, vote like us, live where we do, and see everything like we do. And it also teaches us that anybody who talks, thinks, votes, worships, or sees the world differently than us can't be trusted. They may even be our enemy. This way of seeing the world makes love pretty conditional—with the condition being, *we only have to love people who are just like us.*

The good news is that God isn't like that. Not even close. God's love is unconditional, and it's for everybody. God's love turns enemies into friends, and it is bigger than all the things we cook up to divide ourselves. But God doesn't want to be the only one around here who loves this way. He wants *us* to love this way too. You see, God doesn't want us to love some people, sometimes. He wants us to love everybody, always.

Everybody? Yes, everybody. The people we like and the people we don't? Yes. The people we respect and the people who creep us out? Exactly. The people we admire and the people we don't? Them too. Everybody actually means *everybody*.

Well, what about *always*? Does that mean, literally, always? Yes, it does. As in, when we feel like it and when we don't? Yep. When it's easy and when it's hard? Bingo. When it gives us energy and when it wears us out? Precisely. For God, always really means *always*.

Now, if this sounds like a tall order, you're right. But you're also in luck. God does not leave us to love this way by trusting in our own willpower. The Holy Spirit is around to actually help us love this way. But there's another part too: this is something we can actually train in to get better. Like running a marathon or practicing an instrument, love is something we learn and grow in as we practice. And that's where a study like this comes in really handy.

Everybody, Always is a five-week experiment in learning how to love everybody, always like God does. Each session will explore a different aspect of this love through the teachings and stories of Bob Goff. There will be an opening question, a little Bible reading, and then you'll watch Bob on the video.

However, the real action comes after the video, when you dig in to each topic in a guided small group time. Here we let the rubber meet the road and see how loving everybody, always, gets practical. It's going to be great. Really. However, if you want to get the most out of your *Everybody, Always* experience, it's best to keep a couple of things in mind.

First, the real growth in this study will happen during your small-group time. This is where you will process the content of Bob's message, ask questions, and learn from others as you listen to what God's love is doing in their lives.

Which bring us to point two: small groups can be a deeply rewarding time of intimacy and friendship, but they can also be a disaster. Work to make your group a "safe place." That means first being honest about your thoughts and feelings as well as listening carefully to everyone else's.

Third, resist the temptation to "fix" a problem someone might be having or to correct someone's theology. That's not what this time is for. And finally, keep everything your group shares confidential. All this will foster a rewarding sense of community in your *Everybody, Always* group and give God's Spirit some space to heal, challenge, and empower you to love without conditions.

HOW TO USE THIS GUIDE

As you'll discover throughout this study, love is practical. It gets out there and does things. It takes risks. This study is designed to give you similar opportunities.

Each session in *Everybody, Always* begins with a mixer question followed by a reflection from the Bible. Then you'll watch the video teaching with Bob and jump into some directed small-group discussion. Even though there are lots of questions available for your small group, don't feel like you have to use them all. Your leader will focus on the ones that resonate with your group and guide you from there.

The final component of each session is called "Doing the Word." This is where *Everybody, Always* might diverge from studies you have done before, as your group will engage in one hands-on, practical exercise that makes the content Bob described in the video come alive. These exercises are designed to be completed during your meeting, and they will be what you make of them. If you choose to only go through the motions or abstain from participating in these exercises, there is a lot less chance you'll find what you're looking for during this time. But if you give it a go and take the gamble, you may discover what so many others have already found to be true: *faith comes alive when we take holy risks for God.*

Now, the thought of "risky" activities can make some folks feel anxious. That's okay. If you fall into this category, just read ahead to each "Doing the Word" activity, and you can see what you're going to be invited to try. Then you can prepare yourself accordingly.

And remember, none of these experiments involve anything weird or embarrassing. They are just hands-on opportunities to learn to love like Jesus does.

At the end of each session, there are two or three more opportunities for you to engage the content of *Everybody, Always* during the week. This section includes activities developed around action (called *Do*), Bible reflection (called *Reflect*), and/or reading a short chapter from *Everybody, Always* (called *Read*). The challenge will be to do at least one of these activities between sessions and to use this study guide to record what you learned.

Starting in session two, there will be time before the video teaching to check in about the previous week's activity and process your experiences as a group. If you could not do an experiment one week or are just joining the study, don't worry. Hearing what others have learned will be nourishment enough on its own.

Finally, remember that all this is an opportunity to train yourself in a new way of thinking about love. The videos, discussions, and activities are all meant to kick start your imagination so you start coming up with new ideas and trying things on your own. I mean, what do you think God could do with a whole group of people who were passionate about Jesus' love and eager to put it into creative practice? Let's jump into *Everybody, Always* and find out.

Note: If you are a group leader, there are additional instructions and resources in the back of this guide for leading the activities and discussion times. Because some of the activities require materials and setup, make sure you read this over ahead of time so you will be prepared for each week's activity.

SESSION ONE

LOVE PEOPLE WHERE YOU ARE

We don't need to cross the ocean to love people extravagantly,
we just need to cross the street.

BOB GOFF

GETTING STARTED

Have you ever heard of the musical *Wicked*? It was a big deal when it premiered in 2003, winning all the awards there were to win and making its stars household names. Why was it so popular? Well, aside from amazing songs and great performances, *Wicked* took the story of the *Wizard of Oz* and did something unexpected.

In *Wicked*, the familiar story of Dorothy, the Cowardly Lion, the Scarecrow, and the Tin Man is retold from the perspective of Elphaba, the Wicked Witch of the West. In this telling, we learn about Elphaba's sad backstory, the rivalry with her sister (Glinda the Good Witch), and how she might not be the one-dimensional villain we always thought she was. This musical presents us with an Elphaba who is a tragic figure and whom, we discover, is more misunderstood than mean. It also shows us that when you learn someone's story, it can totally change how you see that person.

In our culture these days, it's tempting to sift everybody we meet into two categories: "good guys" and "bad guys." It is as if life is one of those old vaudeville melodramas where we cheer for the hero and hiss at the villain. But that's not real life, is it? Real life is way more interesting than that. Everybody we know is a fully formed, complex, and interesting creation. Nobody in our orbit is *all* good or *all* bad. Learning people's stories helps us see this. It breaks down our judgments and preconceived notions. It frees us from viewing others as cardboard cutouts but instead as the actual, real, God-created people they are. And, like Elphaba, learning someone's story might help us see them in a different light.

When you get caught up in a life of following Jesus, the old categories of "good guys" and "bad guys" stop working for you. You realize that not only does everybody have a story, but also that God wants us to love them too: *no matter what*. Yes, this can be kind of scary, but that's why we learn people's stories. It makes the creepy people God wants us to love a lot less scary and frees us to actually reach out to them right where they are.

All this is what we're talking about this week in our first session of *Everybody, Always*. We're going to share some stories, learn to reach out to our neighbors, and figure out how to actually love everybody God has already put in our lives . . . always.

CHECKING IN

Welcome to the first session of *Everybody, Always*. If you or any of your fellow group members do not know one another, take a few minutes to introduce yourselves. Then, to get things started, discuss the following questions:

• If you could describe your expectations for this study in one word, what would that word be?

• Why did you pick the word you did?

HEARING THE WORD

Read aloud in the group the following passage from Luke 10:25–37:

25 On one occasion an expert in the law stood up to test Jesus. "Teacher," he asked, "what must I do to inherit eternal life?"

26 "What is written in the Law?" he replied. "How do you read it?"

27 He answered, "'Love the Lord your God with all your heart and with all your soul and with all your strength and with all your mind'; and, 'Love your neighbor as yourself.'"

28 "You have answered correctly," Jesus replied. "Do this and you will live."

29 But he wanted to justify himself, so he asked Jesus, "And who is my neighbor?"

30 In reply Jesus said: "A man was going down from Jerusalem to Jericho, when he was attacked by robbers. They stripped him of his clothes, beat him and went away, leaving him half dead. 31 A priest happened to be going down the same road, and when he saw the man, he passed by on the other side. 32 So too, a Levite, when he came to the place and saw him, passed by on the other side. 33 But a Samaritan, as he traveled, came where the man was; and when he saw him, he took pity on him. 34 He went to him and bandaged his wounds, pouring on oil and wine. Then he put the man on his own donkey, brought him to an inn and took care of him. 35 The next day he took out two denarii and gave them to the innkeeper. 'Look after him,' he said, 'and when I return, I will reimburse you for any extra expense you may have.'

36 "Which of these three do you think was a neighbor to the man who fell into the hands of robbers?"

37 The expert in the law replied, "The one who had mercy on him." Jesus told him, "Go and do likewise."

At the end of this parable, Jesus asks the teacher of the law which of the three people who passed the half-dead man on the road was a "neighbor" to him (see verse 36). Why does Jesus ask this question? Why do you think the expert in the law answers the way he does?

Have you ever seen someone give away extravagant love to a person who was their enemy? If so, when was it and what did it look like?

WATCHING THE VIDEO

Play the video segment for session one. As you watch, use the following outline to record any thoughts or concepts that stand out to you.

Let the people in your life know that they are not only *invited* but also *welcome*.

You do business with *buyers*, but you do life with *neighbors*.

Loving your neighbors is woven into your DNA and your faith.

God's message to you is that you don't have to be afraid anymore.

God gives you a peek at what he is doing in the world through the people around you.

Part of finding your joy in life is helping others find their joy.

God wants you to love everyone, but what you need to do is start across the street.

What's a next big step for you? Who are you going to get to know? What is your next courageous move?

DISCUSSING THE TEACHING

Take a few minutes with your group members to discuss what you just watched and explore these concepts in Scripture.

1. In the video, Bob talks about how he was looking for a *neighbor* rather than just a *buyer* for his house because you "do life" with a neighbor. What does it mean to "do life" with someone? What's an example of this in your life?

2. Do you feel as if you truly "know" your neighbors or just "know about" them? Explain.

3. When you think about your neighbors, what's the hardest (or scariest) part of considering how to connect with them in new ways?

4. Bob states that we find our joy by "helping other people find theirs." What do you think this means? How have you experienced joy through helping others?

5. Is there a difference between joy and happiness? If so, how would you define it?

6. People don't grow where they're *informed*—they grow where they're *accepted*. Where does your small group or church do this well? Where could you all better grow?

DOING THE WORD

For this activity, each participant will need a copy of the grid on the following page and a pen or pencil.

During this week's teaching, Bob suggests that loving your neighbor is something that can start with the people God has put around you in your world. It doesn't require going across the ocean—just across the street.

With this in mind, look at the grid below. This grid represents your neighborhood. The center square with the word "YOU" in it stands for where you live. The empty squares around it represent where your neighbors live.

Take a moment to visualize your neighborhood. Now, see how many of those empty squares you can fill with the actual names of the people who live there. Just do your best. If you live next to the ocean or in the middle of nowhere, just use your office or some other public space where you spend time as your starting place.

It's okay. Just fill in as many names as you can.

YOU

Look at your grid once it's filled in. What do you notice? Are there any trends? Who do you know well? Who do you not know at all?

Next, circle the neighbor on your grid whom you know the least and with whom you want to make a better connection this week. It might be someone you know a little, and you can invite that person to coffee to get to know better. Or it could be a person you don't know at all, and your goal for this week is just to learn his or her name. Whatever it is, take a second, say a prayer, and make your plan.

When you're done, share with the group your plan for connecting with a neighbor this week. If anyone in the group is stumped, offer some suggestions. And remember, the goal here is not to convert anyone, or witness, or anything like that. The goal is just to *connect* . . . because that's where it all starts.

CLOSING PRAYER

Close the meeting by praying for the specific person you are going to try to meet this week. Pray especially that God would give you the courage to follow through!

PERSONAL STUDY

Reflect on the content that you've covered this week in *Everybody, Always* by engaging in any or all of the following between-sessions activities. Remember, this part of the study is not about following rules or doing your homework—the activities are simply designed to give you the opportunity to jump into loving God and your neighbor with both feet. *Please be sure to read the reflection questions after each activity and make a few notes in your study guide about the experience.* There will be a time to share these reflections at the beginning of the next session.

DO: TELL YOUR STORY

During this week's teaching, Bob talks about the power of story and how one of the things that happens when you are neighbors with someone is that you get to know each other better and swap stories. This week, you are invited to do this very thing. Pick one or two people from your small group, get together with that person during the week, and just swap stories. You can get together for a meal, a coffee, or just touch base in the church parking lot. Wherever you do it, your goal is simple: *get to know each other better by sharing a bit of your lives.* Here are a few questions that you can ask to get the stories flowing:

Where did you grow up?

How long have you lived where you do now?

Do you have any siblings? What can you tell me about them?

Who were and are the most formative people in your life?

When and how did you get turned on to Jesus and church?

Why did you decide to participate in this small-group study?

If you had a whole day to yourself, how would you spend it?

What is one thing the two of us have in common?

Once you've connected with one of your group members and shared yours stories, jot down the following reflections to share next week:

How was the experience of sharing stories?

Was it easier or harder than you thought? Why?

What is something this experience taught you about yourself?

REFLECT: BE NEEDY

Read the following passage found in Matthew 18:1–5:

> ¹ *At that time the disciples came to Jesus and asked, "Who, then, is the greatest in the kingdom of heaven?"* ² *He called a little child to him, and placed the child among them.* ³ *And he said: "Truly I tell you, unless you change and become like little children, you will never enter the kingdom of heaven.* ⁴ *Therefore, whoever takes the lowly position of this child is the greatest in the kingdom of heaven.* ⁵ *And whoever welcomes one such child in my name welcomes me.*

One of the things Jesus is always driving home with his followers is that God's kingdom doesn't work like the kingdoms of this world. God's kingdom is counterintuitive. It has a different set of values. Jesus keeps telling those of us who will listen that we will discover this kingdom in ways we least expect.

This section in the Gospel of Matthew picks up a conversation that Jesus was having with his disciples about this very thing. They had just asked him about who was greatest in his kingdom. Essentially, they wanted to know who was the best in God's new world. They were asking, "Jesus, how do you get to the top of the ladder and succeed in your kingdom?" They wanted to know who would—as Bob puts it in the video—"get the big chair."

To answer this question, Jesus asked a child to come over to where they were talking. Then he said, "Be like this." Jesus went on to say that unless the disciples changed to become more and more like this child, they wouldn't even figure out how to be part of what God was up to in the world. What was Jesus getting at by saying this to them?

Well, to live in God's world God's way, we have to first let go of all the ways this current world tells us to succeed. The kingdom of God is a place where the "best" are the least and the lowest. It's where the frail and the fragile are powerful. It's a kingdom of downward mobility, and it's a place people often find when they have failed and are in deep need.

This is part of what Jesus was illustrating with the child he called to stand among him and the disciples. Children have needs. They are not self-sufficient. They are dependent and open to help. It is exactly those qualities that assist us in finding our way into God's new world.

Can you see why a culture that values "pulling yourself up by your bootstraps" might struggle to embrace this message? Success in God's kingdom comes when you stop trying to win and embrace all the ways you keep losing.

What else do you think Jesus meant when he talked about becoming like little children?

Jesus says "anyone who welcomes a child welcomes me." What does that mean to you?

Where are you frustrated by your own need right now?

In what ways might this actually be an invitation into the kingdom of God?

READ: LOVE PEOPLE WHERE YOU ARE

Read the prologue and chapters 1 through 3 in *Everybody, Always*, and then reflect on the following questions:

Who are some people you know who give away love "like they're made of it"? What are some characteristics you admire in these people?

What are some of the barriers you encounter when it comes to loving difficult people? What can you learn from Jesus' example about how to deal with them?

What does "extravagant love" look like in your life in terms of "coloring outside the lines" and "going beyond the norms"?

Why do you think Jesus asks us to start loving others by first loving our neighbors? Who would you define as being your "neighbors"?

What are some ways that you are actively loving your neighbors? How has this involved more than just speaking with them from time to time?

Use the space below to write any other key points or questions you want to bring to the next group meeting. In preparation for your next session, read chapters 4 through 6.

CATCH PEOPLE ON THE BOUNCE

What I want to do is see the hope that's inside of people.

BOB GOFF

GETTING STARTED

One of the most popular TED talks of all time is called "The Power of Vulnerability." It is a talk by Dr. Brené Brown, a research professor who studies empathy and vulnerability.

Dr. Brown has found that empathy and shame are like the opposite ends of an old radio dial. (Remember those?) She says that the way a person moves the tuner on the dial toward either empathy or shame is, in fact, all about how vulnerable that person is willing to be.

For instance, if you turn vulnerability all the way up, you will tune in the "empathy station." On this station, through your sharing of experience, you will find connection with another person. However, if you turn vulnerability all the way down, you will end up tuned in to the "shame station," which just shuts everything down.

Possessing the kind of vulnerability that makes empathy happen is difficult, because you have to open yourself up to other peoples' experiences. You have to be willing to see the world through their eyes and imagine what it's like to stand in their shoes. This costs you something.

However, shame is what happens in the absence of vulnerability. Shame occurs when, because you've been hurt by others in the past, you armor-up, vowing, "That's never going to happen to me again!" As a result, shame produces fear, suspicion, and isolation. So, empathy connects you with other people, while shame drives you further apart.

This week, you will be invited to consider these categories of *empathy* and *shame* when it comes to loving the people in your orbit that you might find a "little creepy." Instead of judging them, you will be asked to consider where they've come from and what they've been through.

Doing this will keep love flowing, and it will put you in the position where you are open to "catching people on the bounce."

CHECKING IN

To get things started for this second session, discuss the following questions:

- What was your first job?

- Do you have good memories or bad memories of the experience? Explain.

Last week, you were invited to act in the in-between sessions personal study.

- Did you meet with one of your neighbors during the week? If so, how did it go?

- Did you do one of the other activities? If so, which one? If not, why not?

- What are some of the things you wrote down in reflection?

- What did you learn about yourself?

HEARING THE WORD

Read aloud in the group the following passage from Matthew 16:13–20:

¹³ *When Jesus came to the region of Caesarea Philippi, he asked his disciples, "Who do people say the Son of Man is?"*
   ¹⁴ *They replied, "Some say John the Baptist; others say Elijah; and still others, Jeremiah or one of the prophets."*
   ¹⁵ *"But what about you?" he asked. "Who do you say I am?"*

> [16] *Simon Peter answered, "You are the Messiah, the Son of the living God."*
>
> [17] *Jesus replied, "Blessed are you, Simon son of Jonah, for this was not revealed to you by flesh and blood, but by my Father in heaven.* [18] *And I tell you that you are Peter, and on this rock I will build my church, and the gates of Hades will not overcome it.* [19] *I will give you the keys of the kingdom of heaven; whatever you bind on earth will be bound in heaven, and whatever you loose on earth will be loosed in heaven."* [20] *Then he ordered his disciples not to tell anyone that he was the Messiah.*

When Jesus calls Peter the rock on which he will "build his church," do you think he is awarding Peter for his answer or naming something about Peter that is already true? Explain.

Why do you think Jesus instructs the disciples not to tell anyone he is the Messiah?

WATCHING THE VIDEO

Play the video segment for session two. As you watch, use the following outline to record any thoughts or concepts that stand out to you.

Instead of telling people what they want, tell them who they are.

Recognize that God made people just like he made you—and he made you to know others.

The best way you can express your faith to people is to tell them who they are becoming.

God found you right where you are, and you can find other people the same way.

The story of the gospel is that Jesus jumped out heaven to be with us.

Talk about the right stuff behind people's backs: who they're turning into, not who they used to be.

Don't let shame distance you from God, and don't let it distance you from others.

Follow Jesus to people who are hurting—who have hit the ground hard—and catch them on the bounce.

DISCUSSING THE TEACHING

Take a few minutes with your group members to discuss what you just watched and explore these concepts in Scripture.

1. In this week's teaching, Bob says we need to stop telling people *what they want* and start telling them *who they are*. What does this mean to you?

2. How do you love difficult people but also have appropriate boundaries with them?

3. What do you think makes it so appealing to say the bad stuff about each other instead of the good stuff?

4. In the video, Bob says that in the end, we're all "turning into love." What questions do you have about that statement? Do you think he's right?

5. Do you agree that showing love "with an agenda" isn't actually showing love toward the people in your world? Why or why not?

6. What does it mean to "catch people on the bounce"? How can doing this give the people in your life a clear view of the hope that Jesus offers to them?

DOING THE WORD

For this activity, each participant will need one 2" x 4" slip of paper, a separate sheet of paper, a pen or pencil, and tape. The group will need one basket or bowl (for collecting the papers).

In the video, Bob stresses how naming what is good and virtuous in others can actually bring those kinds of qualities out of them. So, today, you and your group will give this a try.

Begin by writing your name on one of the 2" x 4" slips of paper the group leader will provide to you. Drop the paper in the basket or bowl that your group leader passes around. Your group leader will then pass the basket around again and invite you to take one slip of paper with another person's name on it. Make sure that if you happen to draw your own name, you put it back in the basket and take a different one.

Next, use the separate piece of paper you were given to write a message to the person whose name you drew. Make sure the message includes one or two things you hope for them as well as anything you've noticed about them that's terrific. You can write a generic message if you don't know the person (such as, "I hope you have a great week," "I pray that you sleep really well every night," or, "I hope you will know how much God loves you"). Or it can be a more specific sentiment if you know the person well.

Once everyone in the group is finished, fold the paper with the message in half. Tape the slip of paper with the person's name on it to the front of the folded paper. Now fold *that* over one more time and return the whole thing to the basket. When everyone has turned in their papers to the basket, your group leader will instruct you to find the slip with your name on it, and then read the note written to you. Afterward, reflect on these questions:

- How did it feel to read the message?

- Did you find it easier to write the message or to read the message? Why?

- Do you want to share your message with the group?

Invite everyone to remember these messages throughout the week and to really "own" them. They represent *who you are* and *who you are becoming.*

CLOSING PRAYER

Close the meeting by praying for specific individuals in your life whom you know have gone through tough times lately or who are dealing with issues of shame. Ask that God would use you to "catch them on the bounce."

PERSONAL STUDY

Reflect on the content you've covered this week in *Everybody, Always* by engaging in any or all of the following between-sessions activities. *Please read the reflection questions after each activity and make a few notes in your study guide about the experience.* There will be a time to share these reflections at the beginning of the next session.

DO: TALK ABOUT THE RIGHT STUFF

In the video teaching this week, Bob suggested that we "start talking behind each other's backs, but talk about the right stuff. Talk about who people are turning into. Say, 'Have you seen Sally? Have you seen who she's turning into?' Or, 'Seen that pastor? Seen who he's turning into?' Find these beautiful things. Talk it up. Don't make it up."

This week, pick three people in your life who represent rings of familiarity on your tree. Start with someone in your "inner" ring who is close to you, like a family member or friends. Next, pick someone who is three rings or so out from that place, such as an acquaintance or someone you meet up with on occasion. Finally pick someone who is four or five rings out from that spot. This could be a person who is distant from you because you don't know him or her well, or because you're critical of the person, or even because he or she is your enemy.

Once you've settled on your three people, write their names in the space provided on the next page. Next, write down three kind, friendly, complimentary statements you are going to make about them behind their backs. You can say these statements to your coworkers, friends, people at church, or anyone else who is at least familiar with the person. Just make sure that you actually say these things to *someone* in your world during the week.

Person #1: _____

Three statements you will make about this individual:

- _____
- _____
- _____

Person #2: _____

Three statements you will make about this individual:

- _____
- _____
- _____

Person #3: _____

Three statements you will make about this individual:

- _____
- _____
- _____

Once you've practiced some good gossip, see how it feels. What was it like? Did it change anything about how you saw the person?

Did it change anything about how you saw yourself? Keep track of your thoughts, make some notes below, and share them next week.

REFLECT: STOP KEEPING SCORE

Read the following passage from Luke 15:11–32:

[11] *Jesus continued: "There was a man who had two sons.* [12] *The younger one said to his father, 'Father, give me my share of the estate.' So, he divided his property between them.*

[13] *"Not long after that, the younger son got together all he had, set off for a distant country and there squandered his wealth in wild living.* [14] *After he had spent everything, there was a severe famine in that whole country, and he began to be in need.* [15] *So he went and hired himself out to a citizen of that country, who sent him to his fields to feed pigs.* [16] *He longed to fill his stomach with the pods that the pigs were eating, but no one gave him anything.*

[17] *"When he came to his senses, he said, 'How many of my father's hired servants have food to spare, and here I am starving to death!* [18] *I will set out and go back to my father and say to him: Father, I have sinned against heaven and against you.* [19] *I am no longer worthy to be called your son; make me like one of your hired servants.'* [20] *So he got up and went to his father.*

"But while he was still a long way off, his father saw him and was filled with compassion for him; he ran to his son, threw his arms around him and kissed him.

²¹ *"The son said to him, 'Father, I have sinned against heaven and against you. I am no longer worthy to be called your son.'*

²² *"But the father said to his servants, 'Quick! Bring the best robe and put it on him. Put a ring on his finger and sandals on his feet.* ²³ *Bring the fattened calf and kill it. Let's have a feast and celebrate.* ²⁴ *For this son of mine was dead and is alive again; he was lost and is found.' So, they began to celebrate.*

²⁵ *"Meanwhile, the older son was in the field. When he came near the house, he heard music and dancing.* ²⁶ *So he called one of the servants and asked him what was going on.* ²⁷ *'Your brother has come,' he replied, 'and your father has killed the fattened calf because he has him back safe and sound.'*

²⁸ *"The older brother became angry and refused to go in. So his father went out and pleaded with him.* ²⁹ *But he answered his father, 'Look! All these years I've been slaving for you and never disobeyed your orders. Yet you never gave me even a young goat so I could celebrate with my friends.* ³⁰ *But when this son of yours who has squandered your property with prostitutes comes home, you kill the fattened calf for him!'*

³¹ *"'My son,' the father said, 'you are always with me, and everything I have is yours.* ³² *But we had to celebrate and be glad, because this brother of yours was dead and is alive again; he was lost and is found.'"*

One of the brilliant truths hanging around this parable Jesus tells is that in life, you will come across people who just seem to be "keeping score." They are the ones who always seem to be writing down all the good that they have done and all the wrongs that others have done. In the story, we've got two brothers and a dad. The younger brother basically tells his dad that he wishes he were dead, and then he leaves town with half of the family money. The younger brothers goes on to waste all that money and eventually winds up in poverty.

Finally, the younger brother comes to his senses and decides to come home to see if he can work for his dad so he can simply eat. But his dad not only welcomes home his younger son but also throws him a huge party to boot. It's an outrageous, even irresponsible, act of mercy.

But there's another brother in the story, and he doesn't like what he sees. This is because the older brother in the parable is a "score keeper." He feels that he has been playing by the rules. He has kept his head down and his nose clean. And he cannot stomach the idea of his dad accepting his young brother back . . . much less throwing him a party!

Perhaps you know a score keeper or two in your life. These are the friends or family members who seem to be walking around with a ledger, always keeping track of the good they are doing and the bad that everyone else is doing. Then, when an opportune moment arrives, they tally the score and remind you of it. If something bad happened to the person on their ledger, they remind you that he or she "had it coming." Or, if something good happened to the person, they complain that "it's not fair," because they've done so much more good in their life.

But in the parable, Jesus turns the notion of "score keeping" on its head. The God character in the story, the father, is ready to celebrate the return of the younger son just because he *loves* him. He hasn't been keeping score of the younger son's wrongs. He doesn't make the son work for him to teach him a lesson, or even make him take any vows to never stray again. The father seems to think mercy is more valuable.

Furthermore, the father's actions demonstrate a way of seeing the world that isn't limited. Not only does he refuse to keep score, but he also doesn't see the need to divide things up equally in order to "make things fair." He doesn't throw the older son a separate party to reward his actions or even acknowledge all the things the older son has been doing. Why? Because everything the father owns already belongs to the son. For the father, it's a limitless world where there's plenty to go around and nobody has to keep score. It's about grace—and grace is not something we earn by following the rules. It's a gift we simply receive.

This is what Jesus invites us to think about with this parable. Do we see the world like the father, or are we more like the older brother? As the older brother stands with his dad, watching the party begin, will he go inside and join it? Will he let go of his scorecard and rejoice in his father's generosity? Or will he stay in his tired old ways of score keeping?

In what ways can you relate to the "score keeping" nature of the older brother?

In what ways has God shown you mercy like he did to the younger brother?

How do you respond to the idea that God doesn't feel the need to divide things equally to "keep everything fair"?

How does this parable challenge you to change your mindset toward others?

Do you think the older brother ever joined the party? More importantly, what would you do if you were in his place?

READ: CATCH PEOPLE ON THE BOUNCE

Read chapters 4 through 6 in *Everybody, Always,* and then reflect on the following questions:

Does your Christian practice feel more like "faith" or "compliance" these days? Explain.

Is there a relationship where you've let shame create a barrier between you and someone else? What would it look like to heal that divide?

What does it mean to build a "kingdom" rather than a "castle" when it comes to accepting others who are different from you?

What are some ways to love the difficult people in your life "thirty seconds at a time"?

Why is it so important to react to those who have failed with compassion and understanding instead of disapproval or indifference?

Use the space below to write any other key points or questions you want to bring to the next group meeting. In preparation for your next session, read chapters 10 through 12.

DON'T PLAY IT SAFE

Playing it safe will steal your joy.

BOB GOFF

GETTING STARTED

Jesus used to really irritate the religious people of his day. They were always getting mad at something he said or did, especially when it came to the poor. One time, some of these folks were questioning Jesus' authority. They thought Jesus didn't have the right to say all the stuff he was saying.

Jesus responded by telling a story (as he often did), and then ended with this statement to the religious elite: "Truly I tell you, the tax collectors and the prostitutes are entering the kingdom of God ahead of you" (Matthew 21:31). As you can imagine, that *really* got under their skin! But why would he say this? Tax collectors and prostitutes were the immoral folks nobody liked. They had blown it and nose-dived in their choices in all the ways those moral religious people hadn't. How could these failures-at-life be plugging into God's world first?

Well, according to Jesus, it was precisely the fact they *had* failed that made the difference. One of the things that gets in the way of us connecting with God is our self-sufficiency. Even if we follow all the rules, do all the right stuff, and pray all the right ways, we can still miss God if we're doing it all by our own strength. This is because we are most open to God when we are needy, busted, and broken. No one knows why it's that way, but that's how it is. It's in our failures that we most easily find God, not in our great achievements.

This is why Jesus said the prostitutes and tax collectors were entering God's kingdom ahead of the "proper" religious folks. They knew all too well what it was like to be broken and needy. Society didn't work for them, and they had been pushed to the edges and looked down on because of it. However, in the great mystery of the gospel, that marginalization is exactly what opened them up to finding grace. And find it they did!

This upside-down dynamic is what this session is all about. It's about getting real enough regarding our own failures to meet the God who wants nothing more than to lavish his grace on us. Yes, this can be scary. And yes, it's a risk. But God can't lavish his grace on us if we don't think we have any needs.

So, what about it? Are you ready for grace? If so, get ready to get real about it all as we jump into this week's teaching.

CHECKING IN

To get things started for this third session, discuss the following questions:

- What is something in your life that you've failed at badly?

- What did you learn from the experience?

Last week, you were invited to act in the in-between sessions personal study.

- Did you "talk about the right stuff" concerning the three individuals you identified? If so, how did it go? How did the people you spoke with respond?

- What are some of the things you wrote down in reflection?

- What did you learn about yourself or about God by engaging in these activities?

HEARING THE WORD

Read aloud in the group the following passage from Matthew 6:1–4:

[1]*"Be careful not to practice your righteousness in front of others to be seen by them. If you do, you will have no reward from your Father in heaven.*

[2] *"So when you give to the needy, do not announce it with trumpets, as the hypocrites do in the synagogues and on the streets, to be honored by others. Truly I tell you, they have received their reward in full.* [3] *But when you give to the needy, do not let your left hand know what your right hand is doing,* [4] *so that your giving may be in secret. Then your Father, who sees what is done in secret, will reward you."*

Why do you think announcing "your righteousness in front of others" is hypocritical?

What kind of reward is Jesus talking about in verse 4?

WATCHING THE VIDEO

Play the video segment for session three. As you watch, use the following outline to record any thoughts or concepts that stand out to you.

If you over-identify with the mistakes you've made and decide to "play it safe," you will miss out on some of the best things God has for you.

Jesus doesn't want you to *show* off your faith—he wants you to *live* out your faith.

You're not defined by your biggest failure. And you're not defined by your biggest success.

Find a safe place to have that discussion where you say, "Here's where the recital went really bad, and here's what I did next."

Instead of moving away from those who have failed, move toward them—not to be nice, *but to be Jesus.*

Can you get real enough with Jesus to admit that you're not fixed yet? Can you honestly say, "I need a second touch from God?"

Failure is what God uses to remind you of your tremendous need for him.

If you're willing to catch people on the bounce—to find those who creep you out and engage with them in love—people will see Jesus through you.

DISCUSSING THE TEACHING

Take a few minutes with your group members to discuss what you just watched and explore these concepts in Scripture.

1. In the teaching, Bob makes the point that Christianity is not like a piano recital: we don't follow Jesus for an audience on

stage. Have you ever been tempted to perform your faith for others? If so, when and where?

2. What does it mean to move toward people who have failed, and not away from them? How does that work?

3. What's the difference between "being nice" and "being Jesus"?

4. Do you know your "blind spots"—those areas in which you may not be perceiving the situation accurately? Who is the person in your life who helps you to see them?

5. Have you ever made a mistake that you have had a hard time getting over? What made getting over it so difficult for you?

6. Do you think this group is safe enough for you to get real to say, "I'm not fixed yet"? Why or why not?

DOING THE WORD

For this activity, each participant will need an index card and a pen or pencil.

For the remainder of this session, you and your group will spend time sharing real stuff and getting honest about your mistakes. As Bob said in the teaching, it's at this place that we meet God and community happens. Start by grabbing an index card and a pen or pencil.

On the index card, write down a mistake you have made that you fear you might be "over-identifying" with. These are the kinds of mistakes that can keep you from jumping toward the life that God has for you—the ones that make you want to stop trying and play it safe by never putting yourself out there again. Be honest. No one is going to read the card but you.

Once everyone in the group has written something down, take the index card you've written and ball it up in your hand. Stand with the group in a circle, and then take two steps back (to make sure everybody has some space). Once everyone is in position, reflect on the trouble this mistake has caused you and the way you realize it has held you. Next, consider if you would like for things to be different.

As everyone in the group is thinking about this, take a jump forward as a way of saying yes to God's invitation of a new life! The jump doesn't have to be big (actually, it shouldn't be—be careful!), and it can also be a step forward if you can't jump or don't have room. Likewise, if you're seated and can't stand, feel free to move a foot or finger forward.

Basically, whatever action you take, make it symbolize your desire to jump toward the new life God has for you and stop playing it safe.

CLOSING PRAYER

As you and the group members stand together in the circle, close by having one person read the words of Psalm 23:1–4 as a prayer and promise from God:

> *The LORD is my shepherd, I lack nothing.*
> *He makes me lie down in green pastures,*
> *he leads me beside quiet waters,*
> *he refreshes my soul.*
> *He guides me along the right paths*
> *for his name's sake.*
> *Even though I walk*
> *through the darkest valley,*
> *I will fear no evil,*
> *for you are with me.*

Say "amen" together and call it a night!

PERSONAL STUDY

Reflect on the content you've covered this week in *Everybody, Always* by engaging in any or all of the following between-sessions activities. *Please read the reflection questions after each activity and make a few notes in your study guide about the experience.* There will be a time to share these reflections at the beginning of the next session.

DO: MOVE TOWARD OTHERS

During the video teaching this week, Bob says, "Instead of moving away from [broken, needy, and creepy people], our idea is to move toward them. Not just to be nice, but to be Jesus." For this week's *Do* activity, you are invited to take a risk . . . and literally move toward folks who are vulnerable and needy.

Identify a place where there are people for whom the systems of our society are not working. This might be a public park, a rescue shelter, a bus station, or anywhere else where people who are intimately acquainted with struggle and even failure might be hanging out. Once you're in this space, just sit and be present for at least thirty minutes.

As you are doing this, pray and ask God to show where he is present—and also evaluate your own discomfort. What are you learning about yourself in this place? What are you learning about these people's struggles? Most importantly, what are you learning about God?

Reflect on your experience, make some notes on the next page, and share with the other group members next week.

What I learned about myself . . .

What I learned about the struggles of the people in this place . . .

What I learned about God . . .

REFLECT: "WHAT'S NEXT?"

Read the following passage from John 9:1–11:

> ¹ *As he went along, he saw a man blind from birth.* ² *His disciples asked him, "Rabbi, who sinned, this man or his parents, that he was born blind?"*
> ³ *"Neither this man nor his parents sinned," said Jesus, "but this happened so that the works of God might be displayed in*

him. ⁴ As long as it is day, we must do the works of him who sent me. Night is coming, when no one can work. ⁵ While I am in the world, I am the light of the world."

⁶ After saying this, he spit on the ground, made some mud with the saliva, and put it on the man's eyes. ⁷ "Go," he told him, "wash in the Pool of Siloam" (this word means "Sent"). So the man went and washed, and came home seeing.

⁸ His neighbors and those who had formerly seen him begging asked, "Isn't this the same man who used to sit and beg?" ⁹ Some claimed that he was.

Others said, "No, he only looks like him."

But he himself insisted, "I am the man."

¹⁰ "How then were your eyes opened?" they asked.

¹¹ He replied, "The man they call Jesus made some mud and put it on my eyes. He told me to go to Siloam and wash. So I went and washed, and then I could see."

One of the things we all like to do when things go wrong is find someone to blame. Whether it's little things or big things, blaming someone else for our troubles is pretty common. People have done it for thousands of years . . . and it's not going away anytime soon. But here's the thing about blaming: *Jesus isn't interested in it.*

In the story above, Jesus runs into a man who has been blind his whole life. Immediately, his disciples ask whose fault it is. Now, this was a pretty common question in Jesus' day. Everyone agreed that a physical disability was someone's fault—they just disagreed as to whose fault it was. So, the disciples are genuinely curious. *Was this guy's blindness a result of something he did? Or something his mom and dad did?* They are asking Jesus to put the whole matter to rest.

However, as Jesus so often does, he transcends the circumstance by inviting the disciples to see how God is working at a whole other level. Jesus explains the man's blindness was neither his nor his parents' fault. Instead, he says, "This happened so that the works of God might be displayed in him." Then Jesus heals him. *Boom.*

Jesus wasn't interested in who was at fault in this man's situation. He knew the disciples were asking the wrong question. And he was attentive to what God was going to do next. This is where it gets interesting for us as well.

When things have gone wrong in our lives, we can spend a ton of time dwelling on whose fault it was and resent the people who we feel got us into this spot. And, to be fair, sometimes we need to do this. Forgiveness and reconciliation can only happen when we name and acknowledge the truths about what has happened to us. However, we can't stay there.

Healing involves moving forward and looking to see what God is going to do next. Our God is a God who wastes nothing. There is no event so sad and broken that he can't bring something new and beautiful out of it. It is what God does, and that's a good thing. The question is whether *we can trust what God is doing.* Can we bring the broken events in our lives to God and trust him to make something beautiful out of them?

Jesus says this is what God does. The question is, do you believe it?

How do you respond to this scene in John 9:1–11? In what ways have you seen people today asking the same question as the disciples?

Where are you feeling the most tempted to look backward and ascribe blame for the hard things in your life?

When was a time when something good emerged out of a sad and tragic circumstance?

Do you think this kind of thing could happen for you again? Why or why not?

READ: DON'T PLAY IT SAFE

Read chapters 10 through 12 in *Everybody, Always*, and then reflect on the following questions:

Why is important to not always be looking for the "green lights" when it comes to boldly stepping out in faith and loving others?

How have you witnessed Jesus helping you to "see more" spiritually as you've continued to follow him?

When has a voice of defeat tempted you to quit what you knew God was leading you to do? How did you respond to that situation?

When you think about the word *evangelism*, does it bring up positive or negative associations? Why did you answer the way you did?

Jesus invites us to move from merely identifying with someone's pain to standing with that person in it. What is the difference between the two? Where is a place in your life that you have an opportunity to "stand in" someone's pain with him or her?

Use the space below to write any other key points or questions you want to bring to the next group meeting. In preparation for your next session, read chapters 14 through 16.

LOOK AT WHAT'S IN YOUR BUCKET

I want to have that new car smell, that new creation smell,
and I think you do too.

BOB GOFF

GETTING STARTED

In Jesus' day, eating with people was a big deal. This is because if you ate with someone, it meant that you were interested in being friends with him or her. It meant you accepted that person, and it was a sign to everyone else in the community about what mattered to you.

Based on this, you'd think that Jesus would have picked all the morally upright, virtuous people to eat with. After all, these were the folks who had been "getting it right" and showing everybody else how it was done. It only makes sense that Jesus would want to point them out by having lunch, right?

Well, you'd be surprised. Or maybe you wouldn't.

Instead of always eating with the rule-following religious people, Jesus often ate with the wrong kinds of people. The people who had blown it. The people who were not respected. The people who were seen as the worst examples of godly living. And here's the thing . . . it drove the religious people nuts.

One time, when these folks asked Jesus about why he did this, Jesus replied, "It is not the healthy who need a doctor, but the sick. I have not come to call the righteous, but sinners to repentance" (Luke 5:31–32).

Of course. Jesus knew that what opens people up to an authentic relationship with God is their *need*. If this sounds familiar (as in, *didn't the last session open with the same lesson?*), you'd be right. It is a major theme in Jesus' ministry. But here's where this lesson diverges from the last one: opening up to God is not just about recognizing your own need but also about moving toward other needy people.

Even the ones you may find a bit creepy.

Here's the thing: if you hang around needy people, you'll find Jesus. No doubt. So the question for this week is, "Do you want to meet Jesus?"

This session shows how it works.

CHECKING IN

To get things started for this fourth session, discuss the following questions:

- Who was your best friend growing up? Where did the two of you meet?

- Are you still in touch? If not, why do you think the two of you drifted apart?

Last week, you were invited to act in the in-between sessions personal study.

- Did you do the *Move Toward Others* activity? If so, how did it go?

- What other reflections do you have to share with the group?

- What did you learn about yourself or about God?

HEARING THE WORD

Read aloud in the group the following passage from John 17:20–23:

[20] *"My prayer is not for them alone. I pray also for those who will believe in me through their message,* [21] *that all of them may be one, Father, just as you are in me and I am in you. May they also be in us so that the world may believe that you have sent me.* [22] *I have given them the glory that you gave me, that they may be one as we are one—* [23] *I in them and you in me—so that they may be brought to complete unity. Then the world will know that you sent me and have loved them even as you have loved me.*

What do you think Jesus has in mind when he prays that all his disciples would be "one"?

Jesus says the unity of his disciples is what will tell the world that he was sent from God (see verse 23). Is the church of today known for its unity? If so, where do you see it? If not, why not?

WATCHING THE VIDEO

Play the video segment for session four. As you watch, use the following outline to record any thoughts or concepts that stand out to you.

You will turn into whatever you fill your "bucket" with. If you fill it with a bunch of love, you'll actually turn into love.

The promise of Scripture is that we each get to be new creations.

If you want more faith, do more stuff—and don't do it because Jesus "needs your help." He doesn't need your help, but he does want your heart.

In John 17, Jesus basically said, "If you want to know what it's like between me and my Dad, just see how people are one—and you can't be one if you aren't engaged."

God grows us up by letting us do things and experience uncomfortable things—because comfortable people don't need Jesus. Desperate people do.

Don't just agree with Jesus. Actually *do* what he said.

Jesus was always available. He had time for *everybody*.

Who's somebody you could engage whom you've been avoiding? Who is somebody who has kind of creeped you out in the past that you could engage?

DISCUSSING THE TEACHING

Take a few minutes with your group members to discuss what you just watched and explore these concepts in Scripture.

1. Are there any difficult people or hard circumstances that have grown your faith? If so, who or what were they? How did you grow from them?

2. How would you describe the difference between *agreeing* with Jesus and *doing* what Jesus said? What does this look like in your life?

3. If it's true that whatever you fill your bucket with you'll become, then what would you most like to fill your bucket with?

4. Is there anything that you need to take *out* of your bucket in order to live the life God has for you? If so, how will you start to do this?

5. We become open to Jesus when we are uncomfortable, afraid, or in need. What would your next "uncomfortable" step be in order to be open to God in a new way?

DOING THE WORD

For this activity, each participant will need five to six slips of paper (nothing larger than 1" x 6"), a Styrofoam coffee cup (or Dixie cup), and a pen or pencil.

During the teaching this week, Bob talks about "buckets" and says that whatever you fill you bucket with, that is what you'll become. Fill it with business deals, and you'll become a business person. Fill it with arguments, and you'll become a lawyer. Fill it with love, and you'll become love. You can fill your bucket with all sorts of good stuff that will help you love others, or you can fill it with all sorts of negative stuff that will get in your way.

So, to close out this time together, you're going to evaluate what's in your bucket. Start by picking up a pen or pencil and one of the cups. The cup represents your "bucket." Next, using the slips of paper provided, write down a few things in your bucket that get in the way of you doing the stuff Jesus is calling you to do. This could be anything from fear, resentments, work, social media, and the like. Just say a prayer, be honest, and write each one down on a separate slip of paper.

Once you're done, stack your slips of paper facedown and set them aside. Remember, no one is going to see this but you. Next, write down two to three things that you *want* to fill your bucket with. These are the things you want to turn into—the stuff that needs to happen in your life to make reaching out to even the creepiest people possible. Once you're done, stack your slips of paper facedown and set them aside. Again, no one should see these but you.

Now, once everyone has their two piles, ball up the slips with the negative stuff written on them, and one-by-one put them into your cup. This is a way of recognizing what's going on in your life now. Say a prayer and take each slip out of your bucket, one at a time. This is a way of saying to God, "I don't want this influence on my life anymore, and I'm ready to get rid of it."

After this—staying in that same place of prayer—take the slips of paper that name what you *want* to fill your bucket with. Again, one at a time, fold them over and place them in your bucket. As each one goes in, let your prayer be one that says, "God, I need more of this in my life. Please help me make that possible."

But you're not done just yet . . . the surprise twist is that you're going take your "bucket" *with you everywhere you go this week.* Let it be a symbol of what you're asking God to do in you and a reminder of the kind of person you want to become! Pay attention to how its presence shapes your attitudes and imagination, and pay attention to how God uses it show you things about him. Take some notes about how it went to share with the group next week.

CLOSING PRAYER

Close the meeting by praying that God would help you "fill your bucket" with the right things. Ask that he would fill your life with his plans so you can become more like him.

PERSONAL STUDY

Reflect on the content you've covered this week in *Everybody, Always* by engaging in any or all of the following between-sessions activities. *Please read the reflection questions after each activity and make a few notes in your study guide about the experience.* There will be a time to share these reflections at the beginning of the next session.

DO: BE AVAILABLE

During the video teaching for this week, Bob notes how he does not send anyone to voice mail. As he says, "People don't follow vision; they follow availability. And there's something beautiful that happens. Every time I pick up the phone and say 'hello,' I've just answered every question anybody has. People just want to know, 'Is it really true?' They want to know that about you, and they want to know that about me, and we can answer that by saying, 'hello.'"

For this activity, simply spend the rest of the week picking up your phone every time it rings. This might seem crazy, but see what God does with it. And if that's too much trouble, then at least try it for a day or even an afternoon. Just take one step toward being available, and see how Jesus meets you there.

Oh . . . and if you don't have a mobile phone, it doesn't mean you get out of this. Do other things to be available, like work with your door open in the office, or eat in the breakroom, or go where people are asking for money on the street and get in a conversation with them. Whatever you choose to do, make note of it below, bring your experiences to share with the group at the next session—and don't forget to take your bucket along.

REFLECT: NOW YOU'RE TALKING

Read the following passage from Matthew 25:31–46:

> [31] *"When the Son of Man comes in his glory, and all the angels with him, he will sit on his glorious throne.* [32] *All the nations will be gathered before him, and he will separate the people one from another as a shepherd separates the sheep from the goats.* [33] *He will put the sheep on his right and the goats on his left.*
>
> [34] *"Then the King will say to those on his right, 'Come, you who are blessed by my Father; take your inheritance, the kingdom prepared for you since the creation of the world.* [35] *For I was hungry and you gave me something to eat, I was thirsty and you gave me something to drink, I was a stranger and you invited me in,* [36] *I needed clothes and you clothed me, I was sick and you looked after me, I was in prison and you came to visit me.'*
>
> [37] *"Then the righteous will answer him, 'Lord, when did we see you hungry and feed you, or thirsty and give you something to drink?* [38] *When did we see you a stranger and invite you in, or needing clothes and clothe you?* [39] *When did we see you sick or in prison and go to visit you?'*

[40] *"The King will reply, 'Truly I tell you, whatever you did for one of the least of these brothers and sisters of mine, you did for me.'*

[41] *"Then he will say to those on his left, 'Depart from me, you who are cursed, into the eternal fire prepared for the devil and his angels.* [42] *For I was hungry and you gave me nothing to eat, I was thirsty and you gave me nothing to drink,* [43] *I was a stranger and you did not invite me in, I needed clothes and you did not clothe me, I was sick and in prison and you did not look after me.'*

[44] *"They also will answer, 'Lord, when did we see you hungry or thirsty or a stranger or needing clothes or sick or in prison, and did not help you?'*

[45] *"He will reply, 'Truly I tell you, whatever you did not do for one of the least of these, you did not do for me.'*

[46] *"Then they will go away to eternal punishment, but the righteous to eternal life."*

This particular passage from Matthew's Gospel is perhaps one of the most complex and confusing in the whole Bible. It's one of those passages that we'd like to just gloss over, because, if we're honest, it kind of makes Jesus look bad. There's sheep and goats, great separations, but also . . . eternal punishment. What is going on here?

The answer is lots of things, but for this study we want to look at one particular part of the parable: the big list of stuff Jesus proclaims that when done to others, it's like doing it to him. You know the list: feeding the hungry, giving the thirsty a drink, welcoming strangers, clothing the naked, caring for the sick, and visiting people in prison. In the parable, Jesus says the criteria of who ends up a sheep or a goat has to do with these lists.

And yet . . . if we have a gospel that is all about grace, unconditional love, and unearned mercy, then doing the right things can't be a way to earn a spot in God's kingdom. If so, it would be the opposite of everything that Jesus had taught up until this point. So, if the lists aren't about that, what are they about?

A while ago, a pastor named Gary Chapman published a book called *The Five Love Languages*. In the book, he talks about how people give and receive love in one of five different ways:

(1) acts of service
(2) words of affirmation
(3) quality time
(4) physical touch
(5) giving gifts

Each of these acts is like a "language" that we use to communicate to others. Using someone's love language is a tangible way to say, "I really care about you."

Is it possible that all these good works Jesus mentions in Matthew 25:31–46—the ones that are on the list—are simply God's *love language*? Might it be the case that the list is not a bunch of things we have to do to try to *earn* God's love but instead are a description of how to live in ways that say to God, "I really care about you"? As Bob noted, Jesus doesn't want our help, but he does want our heart. Maybe this is just the way to give it to him.

What questions does this parable of Jesus bring up for you?

What are some of the ways that people show love to you? And what is your primary "love language" to express care to others?

If God's "love language" involves reaching out to people in all kinds of need, where are you already engaged in that kind of service?

Are there other opportunities for connecting with the needy that God might be calling you to do as well?

READ: DO MORE STUFF

Read chapters 14 through 16 in *Everybody, Always*, and then reflect on the following questions:

When are some times you've seen God leading you from the safest route to the one that helped you grow the most?

How would it change your life if you viewed every person you met as Jesus?

What is Jesus' ultimate "plan" for us when it comes to serving others?

What do you think Jesus meant when he said that if we make a big deal about what we're doing now—hoping someone will clap—we've already gotten our reward?

What has helping others taught you personally about the cost of grace?

Use the space below to write any other key points or questions you want to bring to the next group meeting. In preparation for your next session, read chapters 20 through 24.

LOVE EVEN THE DIFFICULT PEOPLE

God didn't say it would be easy. He just said it would work.

BOB GOFF

GETTING STARTED

So, what does this all mean for us? This is the big question we're asking in this final session. During the last four sessions, we've discussed how loving Jesus doesn't mean we have to cross the ocean, we just have to cross the street. We've seen that the people who creep us out the most are also our neighbors—and loving them means learning their stories. We've learned that doing this kind of thing can be risky, but that in Jesus we can actually become people who take the risk.

All this means there's yet one more step for us to take: *we have to actually do it*. There's a difference between *learning* about how to do something and actually *taking a step* to do it. The plan for this final session is to get you thinking about how you are going to love everybody, always. As we will see, this includes your friends, family, and acquaintances, but it also includes the difficult people you don't normally get along with—who might be called your "enemies."

You've been training for this. All the in-between sessions activities have been designed to grow your imagination and stretch your comfort zone so you can make your own plan for what comes next. So take a deep breath, say a prayer, and jump into this session.

And don't worry. If you blow it a time or two, remember that God will always be there to catch you on the bounce.

CHECKING IN

To get things started for this final session, discuss the following questions:

- How do you respond to this idea of taking steps to love the difficult people in your life?

- What are some challenges that you think you will have in doing this?

Last week, you were invited to take your "bucket" around with you as a reminder of the kind of person you want to become.

- Did you do this? If so, how did it go? What was your experience like?

- Did you do any of the other activities from the between-sessions personal study? If so, which ones?

- What did you learn about yourself? What did you learn about God?

HEARING THE WORD

Read aloud in the group the following passage from Matthew 5:43–48:

> [43] *"You have heard that it was said, 'Love your neighbor and hate your enemy.'* [44] *But I tell you, love your enemies and pray for those who persecute you,* [45] *that you may be children of your Father in heaven. He causes his sun to rise on the evil and the good, and sends rain on the righteous and the unrighteous.* [46] *If you love those who love you, what reward will you get? Are not even the tax collectors doing that?* [47] *And if you greet only your own people, what are you doing more than others? Do not even pagans do that?* [48] *Be perfect, therefore, as your heavenly Father is perfect.*

What is one practical way you've seen someone love his or her enemy?

Since the gospel is all about people who make mistakes and find God in their failure, what do you think Jesus means when he tells his disciples to "be perfect"?

WATCHING THE VIDEO

Play the video segment for session five. As you watch, use the following outline to record any thoughts or concepts that stand out to you.

Your stories, and the way you apply what you've learned about faith to what you've learned in your life, actually have the ability to change people.

If you really want a grade on where you're at in your faith, see how you're treating the people who creep you out.

People who put wheels on their faith are willing to take tremendous risks to do that. Not so they're the hero, or the victim, but so they're a participant.

We don't need to understand everything about forgiveness to get a little of it.

On your very worst day—on that day of your biggest screw-up that you don't want to let anybody know about—God still calls you his *beloved.*

Do you want to be "perfect" bad enough that you're willing get past all the stuff that is keeping you wrapped around the axle?

Instead of trying to figure everybody out, just love everybody.

What's your next step to move a little closer to the Author of love?
What is your next step to move toward loving everybody, always?

DISCUSSING THE TEACHING

Take a few minutes with your group members to discuss what you just watched and explore these concepts in Scripture.

1. Consider Bob's story in this week's teaching about Kabi the witch doctor. What stuck out to you, touched you, or even inspired you?

2. Do you relate to Bob's statement about spending his whole life avoiding the very people Jesus was always engaging? Why or why not?

3. Have you ever been someone else's enemy? Do you know why?

4. Is it easier for you to *forgive* or to *receive* forgiveness from others?

5. What are some healthy precautions to take in dealing with those people who are just unsafe to be around? How can these precautions keep you from being stuck in fear when it comes to approaching them?

6. What is the most threatening part of Bob's challenge to "just do it" when it comes to loving your enemies?

DOING THE WORD

For this activity, each participant will need one sheet of paper and a pen or pencil.

For the past four weeks, you have engaged in the *Everybody, Always* study through group discussion and a practical activity designed to help you learn to love everybody, always. These activities have been provided for you . . . until now! This week, it's your turn.

On the sheet of paper, make a list of your "enemies." Now, these can be *actual* enemies, meaning people who are actively trying to do you harm in the world. They can also be the people you have avoided in the past—somebody from whom you're estranged, or even somebody from whom you've kept your distance because he or she wounded you deeply.

Once you and your group members have completed the list, take five minutes to write beside each name several ways that you can to connect with that person. This could be a social media account, email address, phone number, a common acquaintance—anything will do for a starting point. Next, pick one person on the list whom you will reach out to and love after the study is over. Sketch out your plan on the paper for how you're actually going to do it.

After the five minutes are up, share with the group some of what you've written. Tell the group the person on the list whom you are going to approach. Remember, as Bob says during the teaching, if any of the people on your list are dangerous or unsafe, be smart about all this and ask the group for advice and guidance. The idea is to leave this session with a plan for what your "next step" toward loving others will be.

Use the following questions to close out your time and reflect on the experience of the study as a whole.

Before going through this study, I used to think _____
_____,
but now I wonder _____
_____.

The best thing about this experience was _____
_____.
The worst thing was _____
_____.

If I could describe my *Everybody, Always* experience in one word, it would be: _____.

CLOSING PRAYER

Close the meeting by praying that God would give you the courage to not just *agree* with Jesus but actually go out and *do* what he says. Then pray that God would help you to not allow fear to hold you back in truly loving everybody, always.

PERSONAL STUDY

Reflect on the content that you've covered during this final week in *Everybody, Always* by engaging in any or all of the following between-sessions activities. The time you invest will be well spent, so let God use it to draw you closer to him. Be sure to share with your group leader or group members in the upcoming weeks any key points or insights that stood out to you.

DO: BLESS YOUR HEART

The challenge for this week is to follow up on the "next step" you formulated with your group at the group time. This is part of the grand adventure you are invited into when you follow Jesus! Don't pay your discipleship lip service only. Get out there this week and take that next step! But if you're stuck and don't know how to move toward this goal, here's a place to start.

In the book of Romans, Paul says you should "bless those who persecute you; bless and do not curse" (12:14). One way to live out this teaching is to call to mind one of the "enemies" on the list you made during the group time—the one you find it the hardest of all to love. Then, while you're holding that person in your thoughts, ask that God would bless him or her.

That's it. It's that simple. Except that when you try it, you will probably find that it's not! Offering a prayer of blessing for someone who has hurt you or done wrong to you can feel really weird. But that's because God is using it to grow you and set you free.

Now, you are not blessing the people who are out to get you so they'll have some sort of divine encounter with God (though that would be cool, wouldn't it?). Instead, you are blessing them so *you* can be released from the stuff that clogs your heart—things like hate, bitterness, and resentment. You bless them because it's good for both parties and, on the off chance the opportunity arises for the two of you to reconcile, you'll be ready.

So, go forth and bless their hearts . . . in the name of Jesus.

PRAY: FORGIVE AS THEY'VE BEEN FORGIVEN

Read the following passage from 2 Corinthians 2:5–11:

> *⁵ If anyone has caused grief, he has not so much grieved me as he has grieved all of you to some extent—not to put it too severely. ⁶ The punishment inflicted on him by the majority is sufficient. ⁷ Now instead, you ought to forgive and comfort him, so that he will not be overwhelmed by excessive sorrow. ⁸ I urge you, therefore, to reaffirm your love for him. ⁹ Another reason I wrote you was to see if you would stand the test and be obedient in everything. ¹⁰ Anyone you forgive, I also forgive. And what I have forgiven—if there was anything to forgive—I have forgiven in the sight of Christ for your sake, ¹¹ in order that Satan might not outwit us. For we are not unaware of his schemes.*

Paul has been corresponding with the Corinthian church, and it appears that one of their members did something inappropriate to him. We don't know what it was, but we do know Paul is aware of it and has heard how the community worked through it with the person. As a result, even though Paul hasn't yet reconciled with the offender, he tells the church that the way they forgave the person is all he needs. As of now, he's good. The Corinthians don't need to protect his honor by shaming this guy any more. Their witness of forgiveness is all he needs.

Could there be a more different attitude from what we find today? Holding grudges is like an Olympic sport in our culture. Oftentimes, we're not even holding them against the people who did anything to *us*—we're holding them against people who did stuff to our friends, spouses, or kids. The problem with this is it's not helping. In fact, it's making us sick, because it's forcing us to store up all sorts of resentment and pain in our hearts. We think we're holding the grudge to punish the other person, when in fact we're just hurting ourselves.

So let's follow the example of Paul. If there's somebody who's hard for you to love, don't let a mistake he or she made with someone else be a roadblock for you. You *can* forgive that person.

What strikes you about Paul's words to the church in 2 Corinthians 2:5–11?

Are you currently carrying a grudge about something that happened to a loved one? What is it?

What would need to happen for you to be able to forgive the offender and let it go?

What would you need from God to make that possible?

READ: LOVE EVEN THE DIFFICULT PEOPLE

Read chapters 20 through 24 in *Everybody, Always*, and then reflect on the following questions:

What are some situations you are facing right now where you need to hear God say, "Be not afraid"? What would it take for you to be courageous in that situation?

When are some times that God "blew your mind" and used unbelievable things to help you experience his power?

Every day, we get to decide whether we're really following Jesus or treating him like "he's just a Sherpa carrying our stuff." What is the difference between the two?

When you think about your life, do you tend to look at how far you have to go or see how far you've come? Why do you think you answered like you did?

How have you seen your life change as you've learned to love difficult people? How have you seen your loving actions change another person's life?

LEADER'S GUIDE

Thank you for your willingness to lead a group through *Everybody, Always*! What you have chosen to do is important, and much good fruit can come from studies like this. The rewards of being a leader are different from those of participating, and we hope as you lead you will find your own walk with Jesus deepened by this experience.

Everybody, Always is a five-session study built around video content and small-group interaction. As the group leader, imagine yourself as the host of a dinner party. Your job is to take care of your guests by managing all the behind-the-scenes details so that as your guests arrive, they can focus on each other and on interaction around the topic.

As the group leader, your role is not to answer all the questions or reteach the content—the video, book, and study guide will do most of that work. Your job is to guide the experience and culti-vate your small group into a kind of teaching community. This will make it a place for members to process, question, and reflect—not receive more instruction.

There are several elements in this leader's guide that will help you as you structure your study and reflection time, so be sure to follow along and take advantage of each one.

BEFORE YOU BEGIN

Before your first meeting, make sure everyone in the group has a copy of this study guide so they can follow along and have their answers written out ahead of time. This will keep everyone on the same page and help the process run more smoothly. Alternately, you can hand out the study guides at your first meeting and give the group members some time to look over the material and ask any preliminary questions.

Likewise, encourage each participant (or couple) to also get a copy of the book *Everybody, Always* so they can complete the suggested readings in the in-between sessions personal study, should they desire to do so. If this is not possible, see if anyone from the group is willing to donate an extra copy or two for sharing. Giving everyone access to all the material will help this study be as rewarding an experience as possible. During your first meeting, also be sure to send a sheet of paper around the room and have the members write down their name, phone number, and email address so you can keep in touch with them during the week.

Generally, the ideal size for a group is about eight to ten people, which ensures everyone will have enough time to participate in discussions. If you have more people, break up the main group into smaller subgroups. Encourage those who show up at the first meeting to commit to attending the duration of the study, as this will help the group members get to know each other, create stability for the group, and help you know how to prepare each week.

HOSPITALITY

As group leader, you'll want to create an environment conducive to sharing and learning. A church sanctuary or formal classroom may not be ideal for this kind of meeting because they can feel formal and less intimate. Wherever you choose, make sure there is enough comfortable seating for everyone and, if possible, arrange the seats in a semicircle so everyone can see the video easily. This will make transition between the video and group conversation more efficient and natural.

Also, try to get to the meeting site early so you can greet participants as they arrive. Simple refreshments create a welcoming atmosphere and can be a wonderful addition to a group study evening.

If you do serve food, try to take into account any food allergies or dietary restrictions your group may have. Also, if you meet in a home, you will want to find out if the house has pets (in case there are any allergies) and even consider offering childcare to couples with children who want to attend.

Finally, be sure your media technology is working properly. Managing these details up front will make the rest of your group experience flow more smoothly and provide a welcoming space in which to engage the content of *Everybody, Always.*

STRUCTURING THE GROUP TIME

You will need to determine with your group how long you want to meet each week so you can plan your time accordingly. Generally, most groups like to meet for either sixty minutes or ninety minutes, so you could use one of the following schedules:

Section	60 Minutes	90 Minutes
WELCOME (Members arrive and get settled)	5 minutes	10 minutes
CHECKING IN (Discuss one or two of the opening questions for the session)	5 minutes	15 minutes
HEARING THE WORD (Discuss one or two of the questions in this section)	5 minutes	15 minutes
WATCHING THE VIDEO (Watch the teaching material together and take notes)	20 minutes	20 minutes
DISCUSSING THE TEACHING (discuss the Bible study questions you selected)	25 minutes	30 minutes

As the group leader, it is up to you to keep track of the time and keep things moving along according to your schedule. You might want to set a timer for each segment so both you and the group members know when your time is up. (Note there are some good phone apps for timers that play a gentle chime or other pleasant sound instead of a disruptive noise.)

LEADING YOUR GROUP

If you are new to leading a small group, what follows are some simple tips to making your group time healthy, enjoyable, and effective. First, consider beginning the meeting with a word of prayer. Then remind people to silence and put away their mobile phones. This is a way to say "yes" to being present to one another and to God.

Each of the sessions begins with an opening reflection. The two questions that follow in the "Checking In" section serve as an icebreaker to get the group members thinking about the topic at hand. Some people may want to tell a long story in response to one of these questions, but the goal is to keep the answers brief. Ideally, you want everyone in the group to get a chance to answer, so try to keep the responses to a minute or less. If you have talkative group members, say up front that everyone needs to limit the answer to one minute.

Give the group members a chance to answer, but tell them to feel free to pass if they wish. With the rest of the study, it's generally not a good idea to have everyone answer every question—a free-flowing discussion is more desirable. But with the opening icebreaker questions, you can go around the circle. Encourage shy people to share, but don't force them.

After the "Checking In" time, your group will engage in a simple Bible study drawn from the content of the video, called "Hearing the Word." You do not need to be a biblical scholar to lead this effectively. Your role is only to open up conversation by using the instructions provided and inviting the group into the text. Following this, the group will watch Bob on the video and then answer some small-group discussion questions.

Encourage everyone in the group to answer the questions in the "Discussing the Teaching" section, but make sure that if someone does not want to share (especially as the questions become more personal), he or she knows it is not required. As the discussion progresses, follow up with comments such as, "Tell me more about that," or, "Why did you answer the way you did?" This will allow participants to deepen their reflections and invite meaningful sharing in a nonthreatening way.

Note that you have been given multiple questions to use in each session. You do not have to use them all or follow them in order. Feel free to pick and choose questions based on either the needs of your group or how the conversation is flowing. Also, don't be afraid of silence. Offering a question and allowing up to thirty seconds of silence is okay. It allows people space to think about how they want to respond and also gives them time to do so.

As group leader you are the boundary keeper for your group. Do not let anyone (yourself included) dominate the group time. Keep an eye out for group members who might be tempted to "attack" folks they disagree with or try and "fix" those having struggles. These kind of behaviors can derail a group's momentum so they need to be shut down. Model "active listening" and encourage everyone in your group to do the same. This will make your group time a "safe space" and foster the kind of community that God can use to change people.

The "Doing the Word" time that concludes the session will be the most dynamic part of this study. During this section, participants are invited to put what they have learned into practical action. However, for this to be successful, it will require some preparation on your part. Take time to read over each session's "Doing the Word" activity, as several of them require special materials. Reading ahead will allow you to ask group members to bring any items you might need but don't have and will give you a sense of how to lead your group through these experiences. Use the supply list below to make sure you have everything you need.

Supply List

Session 1: _Love People Where You Are_
- Copy of the "YOU" grid for every participant
- Pens or pencils

Session 2: _Catch People on the Bounce_
- One 2" x 4" slip of paper (for everyone to write his or her name on)
- Additional notebook or typing paper for each participant
- Pens or pencils
- Basket or bowl (for collecting names)
- Tape

Session 3: _Don't Play It Safe_
- Index cards (enough for everyone in the group to have one card)
- Pens or pencils

Session 4: _Look at What's in Your Bucket_
- Five to six small slips of paper (nothing bigger than 1" x 6") for each participant
- Styrofoam coffee cup or Dixie cup (you will need one for each participant)
- Pens or pencils

Session 5: _Love Even the Difficult People_
- One sheet of paper for each participant
- Pens or pencils

Finally, even though there are instructions for how to conclude each session, please feel free to strike out on your own. Just make sure you do something intentional to mark the end of the meeting. It may also be helpful to take time before or after the closing prayer to go over that week's between-session personal study options and ask people what they would like to try. This way, everyone can depart in confidence.

GROUP DYNAMICS

Leading a group through *Everybody, Always* will prove to be highly rewarding both to you and your group members. However, this doesn't mean you will not encounter any challenges along the way! Discussions can get off track. Group members may not be sensitive to the needs and ideas of others. Some might worry they will be expected to talk about matters that make them feel awkward. Others may express comments that result in disagreements. To help ease this strain on you and the group, consider the following ground rules:

- When someone raises a question or comment that is off the main topic, suggest you deal with it another time, or, if you feel led to go in that direction, let the group know you will be spending some time discussing it.

- If someone asks a question you don't know how to answer, admit it and move on. At your discretion, feel free to invite group members to comment on questions that call for personal experience.

- If you find one or two people are dominating the discussion time, direct a few questions to others in the group. Outside the main group time, ask the more dominating members to help you draw out the quieter ones. Work to make them a part of the solution instead of the problem.

- When a disagreement occurs, encourage the group members to process the matter in love. Encourage those on opposite sides to restate what they heard the other side say about the matter, and then invite each side to evaluate if that perception is accurate. Lead the group in examining other Scriptures related to the topic and look for common ground.

When any of these issues arise, encourage your group members to follow these words from the Bible: "Love one another" (John 13:34), "If it is possible, as far as it depends on you, live at peace with everyone" (Romans 12:18), and "Be quick to listen, slow to speak and slow to become angry" (James 1:19). This will make your group time more rewarding and beneficial for everyone who attends.

Thank you again for your willingness to lead your group. May God reward your efforts and dedication and make your time together in *Everybody, Always* fruitful for him.

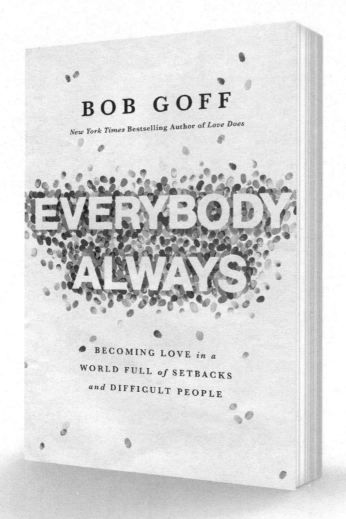

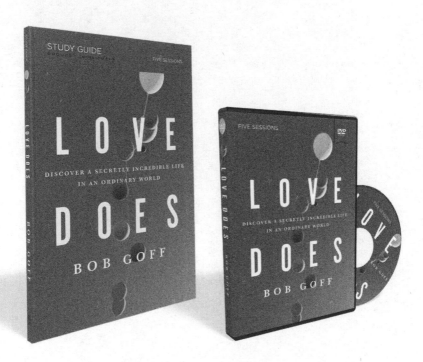